T0171496

Higher Places

A Compilation of
Personal Experiences and Growth

PAT D. REAGAN

WESTBOW
PRESS
A DIVISION OF THOMAS NELSON

WestBow Press books may be ordered through booksellers or by contacting:

WestBow Press
A Division of Thomas Nelson
1663 Liberty Drive
Bloomington, IN 47403
www.westbowpress.com
1-(866) 928-1240

Because of the dynamic nature of the Internet, any web addresses or links contained in this book may have changed since publication and may no longer be valid. The views expressed in this work are solely those of the author and do not necessarily reflect the views of the publisher, and the publisher hereby disclaims any responsibility for them.

Any people depicted in stock imagery provided by Thinkstock are models, and such images are being used for illustrative purposes only.

Certain stock imagery © Thinkstock.

ISBN: 978-1-4497-6585-9 (sc)
ISBN: 978-1-4497-6586-6 (e)

Library of Congress Control Number: 2012916254

Printed in the United States of America

WestBow Press rev. date: 09/07/2012

Table of Contents

A Collection
of Inspirational
Short Stories

The Tree Gift

The large tree has always been there at least for the time I could remember. It was such a presence in the backyard. And I saw this Bradford Pear tree everyday. I watched it unveil its beauty each season with the small white flowers at the beginning of spring. It looked like hundreds of white cotton balls on a huge tree. Then the leaves turned from mint to a darker green in the summer. The shade which covered about half of the yard was a welcome rest from the ninety degree heat at the peak of summer. And then during fall the array of colors began. It was first a mixture of yellow and gold. Then some magenta and darker shades of rust and brown came through. I specifically bought a camera to take pictures of this autumn event. The tree was stately, and in the winter I called it a stick tree. It was always there, until hurricane Katrina.

I returned after the storm to find most of the tree on the ground. There was only a small part of it standing. The tree cutter that weighed the yard damage said it would not be right again. Then together we decided to finish what the storm had done and cut the rest of it. That was something I think I did in a mild state of shock.

However, the stump that is still there is a reminder of my tree friend. Sometimes I will go out and sit on that stump just to feel the closeness of the tree. It just makes me feel better.

When the tree movers took it off, I watched as they loaded it on a truck. I just repeated "I am sorry" and wept. It was hard to see it go. For awhile, I did not want to look out back. It was just too hard to see what had been there. So time passed, and I told myself that somehow I would get over it. I had other smaller trees, and I would appreciate them. It was just that this was a beautiful tree, and one I connected with. I felt the loss for months.

Then one morning at sunrise I awakened. This was not my usual routine. However, I pulled the shade in my room, and I gasped at the sight. The horizon was shades of pale pink, orange, and light blue. I stared in silence at what looked like a painting. It was something I had not seen because the huge tree had blocked the view. It was new after all the years. I started getting up early each day just to see the new sunrise and the new picture it would be everyday, and it was different. No two were the same, for the weather and seasons all contributed to the variety of what I saw.

Then I began to realize that the beauty of what I was seeing was made available by the tree leaving. It made me think again that sometimes what you lose is important at the time, but in the "big picture" there is often gift. I am grateful for the time I had with my tree friend, but what I received was a new beginning of my relationship with nature.

The Blue Chair

The blue chair was a necessary purchase. It seemed like a perfect solution to what my mother needed for being in a nursing home. I wanted to provide her with a comfortable place to sit many hours a day since she no longer walked. This was due to a state of dementia that had taken her to a limited world. What I tried to do was make her life more tolerable. I happened to see a dark blue recliner chair at a nearby store. I immediately thought it was appropriate and delivered it myself. The comfortable chair became her identity the day she sat in it. It was a place for us to have our talks and became the center of our visits. We watched television from the chair and looked at magazines and books. She had some dolls, jewelry, stuffed animals, and small pillows to look at. The chair was a special place of security and protection. We filled it with throw pillows and blankets to keep her warm. I saw her most of the time in the blue chair.

After two years, I noticed that the footrest was not working, and some of the cushioned support was gone. I made a decision to replace it and found a new recliner with a lever mechanism for options and adjustments.

As I moved the old chair out and the new one in, I felt like I was losing something special. I took it home, and a neighbor said they would take it to their camp. The positive aspect of moving the chair to a new place gave me a kind of hope for it. It had served loyally all that we needed. I had my little ceremony, just the chair and myself and told it how much it had meant to both of us. I gave it one last hug of appreciation and walked away. It was at my neighbor's house when I left it on a patio getting a good breeze and lots of sunlight. I left on an errand, and when I returned it was gone. The family had picked it up. I felt an emptiness I had not known I would feel. It seemed like the months and years I spent with the chair were associated with my relationship with my mother.

The new chair does not have the character yet. The memories of the blue chair are plentiful, and I will always have them. Keeping it would have only been half of what it was supposed to be because my mother would not have been there. Go to your home blue chair and have a better life. You were always there for us, and what a rightful place you provided. You deserve something more. A new story begins. I will call it "The Brown Chair."

Robin Company

꿍

A long and cold winter with unusually cold temperatures hit the southern states in 2007. Previously, we were used to a warm and cold climate with no consistent cold. That is until this year. I realized that this one would be different when I turned on my heating system, and there was no let up the next day as it had been. I decided to ride out the temperatures and wear layers, sleep under my down comforter and keep the heat going.

What I did not expect was that the flowers would bloom in January during a rare warm spell. Therefore, all the camellias bloomed, other flowers began to blossom, and all was confused, even me. I began to think that nature would right itself, and we could look forward to a real spring.

What I did not count on was the silence of the winter. When this one arrived, I settled in for it. The days were short, and before I knew it they were over. The days meshed into weeks and months. I was counting on the calendar when daylight savings time would come. Although my winter was mild in comparison to the northern states that have been snowbound, this one was a new experience for me. I did not know how much I had hibernated until the sixteenth of February. That day changed it all.

I remember going somewhere, and upon returning I was shocked to see about two hundred robins in the backyard. They were eating red holly berries from a large bush. They flew in all directions from tree to tree as if looking around. It was spectacular to see how they had some system to what they were doing.

They were all beautiful colors of rust, gray and black and looked healthy and well fed from their travels.

The next day I awoke to find them back at the berry bush. Some had scattered, but there were still about seventy-five around the yard. I immediately studied their migration route from the internet and decided to report my sighting for the web site that tracks the migration for many types of birds. They continued to fly around in the morning. Around 2:00 p.m.

central time, they banded together and flew away in a northwest direction. These birds became company for me after a long and silent winter. I hoped all would be well for them on their journey.

The next morning I awoke to see at least fifteen robins back at the berry bush. They continued to stay in that spot for awhile. Then they moved around the yard and flew in the trees. It was if they had decided to stay. I put water in my bird bath because I read that robins liked to take baths. If they wanted to stay, I would help them make my home their home. It was such a joy to see the birds arriving. I now feel that spring is around the corner and appreciate nature and all things that fit into the seasons. I never thought I would value robin company, but they arrived out of nowhere and brightened my gray winter world. What joy I felt when they came, and what sadness I felt when I thought they were all gone. I realize that they came for me to have a greater appreciation of God's work, and He left just enough robins for me to enjoy. After endless dreary days, the robins brightened my spirits. I will welcome those who stayed and enjoy their company, and wish the others who left safe travels.

A Special Place

❧

Long ago as I was learning to play piano it was some work. Later as I grew older it was more fun because it was enjoyment. There were days of practicing for my pleasure instead of for a teacher. It took awhile for the real appreciation to set in. But once it did, I was hooked.

Another way of seeing how music has affected my life is that I feel better when I am involved with either listening or playing. It puts you in a better place of awareness, joy, and peace.

For those who are not there yet, it should be a discovery. Tapping into a wonderful dimension is the gift. It is like the feeling you get being in the presence of good souls.

I have continued to enjoy my music and to play for friends and myself. The reward is so uplifting that only those who are part of this journey can understand. We all nod our heads in, "Yes, we get this."

But to enjoy it ourselves is not enough. We were given these talents to share and to help others move to a happier place. Offering these gifts is much more gratifying than playing for myself. There are times when I seem to be in quiet devotion with my music, and other times when I especially want to share.

Much of my music collection is older and quieter than what I hear today. But, I like it that way, and it is more comforting. I have found that those who are on a path to expression seem to do well in music because there is so much to express.

One time someone reviewed my playing and said, "You have it all together except expression. That changed my perception. I thought, "What have I been missing?"

I delight in bringing this special feeling to others. I know how special I feel myself. In today's world there is no substitute for the enjoyment of good music because it brings good feelings. Anyone can participate just by listening.

In our fast world, do not leave out your uplifting music. It is a support system. Self-care is important.

I don't know how I could live without all my music interests. They are such a part of me and now my "expression". Music is inspirational, it is my heart, and it puts me in a special place.

The Perfect Day

———————— ❧ ————————

S omewhere around mid October there is a blend of sunshine, cool breezes and clear skies. They make up the combination for rest.

After summer heat, it is peaceful to be outdoors with fresh, cool air.

The nature surrounding all these weather autumn symphonies is the added touch. Birds come out, fly, and go from tree to tree. Squirrels scurry about looking for nuts or berries. Orange and yellow butterflies seem to be floating in the special air. Large black crows fly overhead together in some kind of motion. It is such a good day for watching anything. I decided to be a spectator at this event by getting a chair and sitting outside all day, and what a day it was! Seeing animals and birds fitting in a type of unison is spellbinding in the nature world. They were separate, yet together in my space. The light breeze was just enough to be comfortable, so I had drinks, lunch, and a snack outside. It was a picnic for myself.

The other part of this day's intrigue is that afternoon sun is special. I have light and joy all around. Many winter days there is no sun and no way to be outdoors. Many summer days there is intense sun, and it is too hot to be outdoors. The spring is a mixture of wind and light sun and rain. But autumn is the season with just the right day, and it can be a perfect day. We can have many of those days for a few short months. It does not last long, so I cherish these perfect days. Also when they arrive, I can be thankful for nature. When I hear the birds sing on these days, I know they are happy, just as I am. There are always flowers blooming of some sort. I can pick a few to bring indoors to brighten my already sunny kitchen. I am happier when there is more brightness.

When I see the sun setting, I know this special day is over. Tomorrow might be the same because it is that time of year. I look forward to another day. My routine will be similar because I do not want to miss a thing. It is an adventure being surrounded by those who live with me.

My welcome friends, the perfect weather, and calming nature made this a perfect day.

The Dove Pair

Early one October morning, I glanced out a back window of the house to see the sun coming up in the east. The yard looked like it always does, and as I turned away something caught my attention. It was an unusual sight. Two doves were sitting up in a small pine tree on one of the branches. It was obvious they were a pair, one bigger than the other. I sat in a chair with binoculars to see what they were doing since I had never seen them before. They were fat birds; a pale, light gray color. As I watched they were comfortable on their perch. Occasionally I would see a few feathers fly to the ground as they scratched themselves. I suppose it was something doves do. They stayed there for almost an hour very intent on what they were doing. I wondered how long they would stay there. I remained in my chair on watch. After awhile, the smaller bird moved forward to the end of the branch. I decided that was her cue to the other bird to say, "Let's get going." The male bird simply followed her lead. Suddenly they spread their large wings and flew up to a taller tree. They left the tree and flew away.

I wondered why they came. Some say doves bring love from the spiritual world. If that is true, I felt like I had some special company that day. After they left, I went out in the yard and picked up the feathers that were on the ground. I will save those beautiful feathers as a reminder of their visit. I said to myself. "What a wonderful gift today!" I'll look at those feathers when I need some comfort.

I went back to the window several times during the day to see if there was any sign of them, but they were gone. It was just a short visit, but a special one. The last time a dove was here was twenty-five years ago. They rarely come, but when they do it is something that can touch your soul.

Reunion with the Chinese Jar

—— ❧ ——

When I began sorting through things from the family home, I discovered the copper collection amounting to nine pieces.

I knew I did not want them since they were for decorative purposes.

Several years went by, and I did not want to part with this collection. Then one day I made a thoughtful decision to put them in an auction. Surprisingly they sold. I thought it was best for someone else to enjoy and use these items.

After that experience, I looked at other things to clean out. I found a porcelain Chinese ginger jar that had been bought at an antique store. It looked like something that might sell.

The auction did not want it since it was not in the category of the copper, so I found a consignment store. They readily accepted it.

From week to week I called to ask if it was sold. They said, "No."

Then after three months they said I should renew it or pick it up.

I renewed it for three more months hoping it would sell. Inside the jar was a sales receipt so I knew when, where it was bought and the price paid. The store was no longer in business. It seemed that I did not need that jar. It was blue and white and had occupied a space on some shelves. When the time came for me to check the last week of the six months on the jar, the store clerk said it did not sell. It was time to come get it. So, that is what I did. I still do not understand why some things sell and others do not.

Sometimes I see this jar and wonder why I took it away. I think it refused to go. My mother bought that jar years ago. This jar would not leave. I think it is her way of saying to me, although I am gone, I am still with you. You will have a memory of me associated with the Chinese jar. That was a stubborn jar, but it certainly was a reunion.

Liberated from Circles

❧

Many times in my life I have made the comment that life is hard. We came here to learn lessons.

One day while I was laying out in my mind all my needs, I became aware. This was a rehearsal I have done over and over. It was a circle of nowhere.

I began to see that **money** was something that keeps us all trapped in the survival mode. It is faith instead of fear that should direct us. We have been sustained anyway this far. How could we be abandoned unless by our own decisions and lack of effort? I checked this one off the list. That was a big relief.

Then I looked at the issue of **interests**. How can I not be bored? What can I do for entertainment? How can I afford to do the things I want to do? Over and over this was an item. Then I decided I can be content, and that my interests should be selective. I am placed here for now, and have learned that I do not need a lot of interests to be happy.

Also I know that I am **cared about** and do not need a lot of relationships. Quality family and friends are great, but I saw that it is time to transcend a dependency on others.

I sense that I have a **mission or higher purpose.** But until it is revealed to me, I should be content. Learning about being content in your circumstances is a great lesson. I hope I can delete the lists and just "be." I do not want checklists or criteria to be happy. True peace is not related to circumstances. I had some enlightenment suddenly, and this is a step toward a new beginning for me. I feel released from the old circles, and am grateful to be liberated from it.

Being content is a key, and allowing life to unfold is not only the safe way to live, but the way to be directed. Time to see that we are really agents of divine will.

Cry of the Terns

———— ❧ ————

I saw this painting years ago hanging on a wall in my childhood home.

It was just a black and white lithograph and did not seem too special. I preferred color. As time went on, I noticed one day as I was studying it that the birds were actually flying. This picture was hard to ignore as much as I wanted to. It seemed to be speaking to me in subtle messages, "See me and understand me." I am not much of an artist, so I told myself that it would occupy a space. I would live with it since it was a gift passed on to me. What was so important about a painting anyway? I had others with grass and flowers, scenes, poppies, and beautiful stories to tell. I liked them more.

One day I began to sense that the flying birds meant something to me, but I did not know what. To make it more complicated, they were flying over snow covered mountains. We hardly get snow in the southern states. I could not relate at all.

I continued to partly study and partly ignore this art until late one afternoon I decided to sit quietly and look at it. What was it telling me? I was determined to unfold this mystery. I found out that it was not inexpensive, so I decided to keep it for the value.

What other reason would I need?

I began to identify with nature and seasons. I was growing in a way that seemed natural to appreciate birds flying over the mountains. Every step of the way I tried to piece together what that painting meant and even changed its place on walls to get some perspective. I used a lot of ways to rationalize this story.

It occurred to me that this was not about my connection with nature, but about me. I needed to stretch and expand myself. I began to see more of a partnership with the birds. Finally I could rest in the revelation that I needed to become more. Until then, I was satisfied. The birds are now my example to guide me above what was my old life. I have no more doubts about the meaning of Cry of the Terns. It was a way for me to learn more about myself, to fly, and to look to higher ways of living. I hope I can some day soar above the mountains and feel the joy that it brings. It looks like such fun!

The Moonstone Pendant

When I became interested in gemstones, I wanted to learn their meanings. In a book I discovered that they have certain qualities as well as beauty. Some spoke to me and others did not. I collected a few and enjoyed wearing them. Once I bought a sugilite ring and did not know it was coming from Asia. I thought I was ordering from a U.S. website. The tracking number showed that it was in Alaska as the first stop in our country. I wondered if I would ever receive it.

But one day a Fed-Ex truck stopped, and there it was. It was just what I wanted. The quality was more than for what I could have asked.

Learning about gemstones is one of my hobbies. There is something exciting about wearing part of nature. I call it grounding myself.

I needed to learn this because for a long time I wanted to do things my way.

Later I ordered a moonstone pendant to put on a chain I already had. Again, I was not disappointed. The small stones are put together in one design that is one of a kind. At any time I can see a certain pale light blue glow coming from the pendant. So many people have asked me what it is. I reply, "It is moonstone, and it has a glow." They all agree. This pendant represents my recent life. For many years I looked at what I was doing with my decisions. They were trial and mostly error decisions. When I made mistakes one after another, I decided that I might not be the best judge of what to do.

In reading books about surrendering yourself to a higher power and not trying to do things yourself, it occurred to me that I needed to be led. This is a hard one to get. I thought I could control my own life, but when one door closed, I saw another one open, and it was better.

Now I am under the impression that I need to be guided as to what is best for me. After some years of developing this way of life, I continue to go with the everyday flow and see what happens. One benefit of living this way is that I know I am protected and have someone watching over me. That is good to know.

The gems are special to me because they represent a support because of their meanings. The moonstone means inner growth and strength and new beginnings. I am always open to the new in my life and eagerly wait for what is next. When I do not determine my life in a controlling way, I free myself to rest and peace. I can let the master planner take care of that.

Moonstone has a quality of glow and light around it. If I can reflect something of that small spark to others in a piece of jewelry, it is an opportunity to demonstrate joy. I like to see the expressions on faces of people who look at the moonstones. They know it is special. I purposely wear it because it expresses light and lifts spirits.

The Bird Feeder

Every January I bring out the bird feeder. After I stock up on a supply of bird feed for the next three months, I am ready to go with this project. I hang it in a tree where I can look out the window every day and see the activity. There are many varieties of birds that come once I set the feeder out. Sometimes I get a close-up look through my binoculars. It is fun to watch these birds come around for the winter months. When spring arrives, I take the feeder down since there is so much else for them to eat. Spring brings an abundance of everything especially for the birds.

The day after I set the feeder out, I thought about how the birds flocked to it and seemed to be enjoying the feed. Then it occurred to me that the day before they did not know that the large amount of feed was coming the next day.

They were going to be all right no matter what I did. However, it was a help to them on the cold days.

They never know if and when a person will set out food. But they do not seem to care or depend on it.

I learned a lesson that day. If the birds can carry on and take care of themselves without a guarantee of tomorrow why can't I? I now know that faith is important. People need to take a direction from the birds. They are taken care of anyway, and if an abundance comes their way they flow with it. I was glad when I gave them a chance to not have to search for food. It was my gift to them. If I trust I will be taken care of, I can rest in belief that it will be so.

They did not know my gift was coming that day. I will not know if a gift will be coming to me one day. But, I can relax and enjoy my life for what is and trust that a helping hand is there for me just like it was for the birds.

I concluded that birds have no worries. They soar in the skies so peacefully enjoying themselves. Also when I see them on the ground, they are present with what they are doing. Even the ones who wind up on top of a roof or tree seem to like the view. What a wonderful way to live I decided. I thank the bird feeder for my lesson and also the big community of birds in my trees.

The River and the Helicopter

———— ❧ ————

I dreamed I was standing beside a very wide rushing river.

The scene was not for leisure or beauty. It was a challenge. I thought how I might cross this river and actually needing to.

Sometimes in thought one can problem-solve, and this was an opportunity to do so. There were two choices. One was a long, rickety bridge which looked unstable. The thought of falling into a deep river from that bridge was enough for me to think about the other way. It was a small rowboat by the bank of the river. That also looked overwhelming to me because of fast flowing water that I did not think I was strong enough to handle. Perplexing as it was, I was imagining how to get across. Both ideas were dangerous, and neither seemed right. "How could I manage to get over to the other side and still be okay?" I deeply thought.

Having studied the two scenarios, I decided to wait and ponder this problem some more. It occurred to me that I should not accept the bridge or the rowboat because there was so much doubt with each one.

Then a revelation came. It was a cluster of trees nearby that looked interesting. This grouping of tall trees was hiding something. As I moved toward this direction, I noticed that something bright and shiny was behind the trees. To my amazement it was a modern day helicopter just sitting there all by itself. As I approached, there was no one around. I wondered why a helicopter was out there in the trees with no pilot.

As I sat on the grass and waited for awhile, I heard a sound coming in my direction like footsteps. When I looked around, it was a man who came forward. His only words to me were, "Do you want a ride?" From an intuitive feeling, I immediately knew that he was there to help. My problem of crossing the river the other two difficult ways was over.

Now we could fly across in fifteen minutes. What a solution to a complex and discouraging situation! After reaching the other side of this river, I thanked the pilot. He said goodbye and left. He had helped me reach my destination. I learned when something seems difficult and the choices you are facing are not the best, it might be better to **wait** for another answer. And that answer might be **hidden** for awhile until another one seems right. At this point it might be **easy** to work it out. To believe that something right could happen gives strength to the wait. I know I was waiting for the pilot to show up, and he was my answer.

One Stained Glass Piece

❧

The stained glass window at the church is beautiful with many colors of red, emerald green, royal blue, turquoise, white, brown, gold, and yellow. It is impossible not to see and study it when in service. One can only feel good when viewing this work of art.

At first I thought that the window was a way to bring the people to a better place when worshipping. That is true, but I wanted the window to be more than that to me.

As the weeks went by, I enjoyed the window, and all it had to offer.

Perhaps being there and feeling special was all I needed from the window. It was such a warm feeling every Sunday to be in the presence of all the colors especially when the sunlight came from a good direction.

Church for me was about the message, the music, and the appreciation of the window that looked like it was hundreds of pieces of glass put together in a puzzle. Looking at it was amazing because I thought about how all those pieces came together to form a picture. Liking aesthetic things, I could value this wonder.

One Sunday I could not help but be mesmerized again by the light that was reflected through the colors. Suddenly I felt like all the pieces had come together to make this picture. The pieces alone and separate would have meant nothing.

It occurred to me that if I could be like just one piece of the picture, one piece of glass, and one of the colors to make up the whole, what a great role to play. The pieces of colored glass making up a spectacular window for a church are important I reasoned.

I walked out that day with a different attitude. I would like from this day forward to be like one piece of the picture. If I can contribute something that beautiful in my daily walk along with others, then I will feel like I answered a call.

Hi Angel

❧

We have all seen them before. They are the men or women standing outside a store ringing a bell to collect money for the Salvation Army.

The red kettle hanging there indicates their mission. I usually put a few coins in when entering a store.

One day as I was approaching a market to buy food, I saw something different. This time a man bundled up in a coat, hat, and dark sunglasses was there. I did not know what to think. It seemed a bit concerning that he looked like something out of a movie that spoke loudly, "Be cautious!" I decided to carefully go up to the kettle and drop in my money and pick up a fast pace inside. This did not feel too comfortable. That was my plan.

Others went by simply ignoring him possibly by the way he looked. I wanted to be better, so I pulled out all my courage and walked up to him. The coins went into the kettle, and he looked thankful.

I felt good about what I did instead of avoiding him and losing out on my opportunity to give.

As I was walking away, he smiled broadly and said, "Hi Angel!" I replied, "Hello" and went inside the store.

I am not sure what his job was that day. One thing I know for sure was that he was glad to see me. Judging from the lack of response, I might have made his day. The most interesting thing about all this was what he said to me. It really made my day when he called me an angel. This is big upgrade to be called that especially from a stranger. I thought, "Could I be someone a perfect stranger sees as an angel or have angelic qualities?" I like to hope so. It inspired me to look at myself in a capacity of what I could be. Perhaps a more comforting and compassionate person would be a good start. I waved to him as I left the store, and he waved back and smiled.

I have heard that sometimes we encounter angels and do not realize it. I know I learned something from him that day and was glad

I went shopping. The curious part of that meeting that still remains with me even today is that I have wondered who that man really was.

The Sunset and the Star

꿍

One late afternoon as I was driving home, there was a beautiful sunset. The night air was cold in winter. The sky was clear, and I was going west toward the sunset. It was somewhat light out in the direction I was going. There were lights on the cars going both east and west that were sharing the four-lane highway with me.

I was listening to a calming CD in my warm car when I looked up in the clear dark blue sky. Among the colors of the sunset which were pink, orange, and gold, there was one and only one star in the sky to my left. I thought, "Where are the others?" Perhaps they are there, and I cannot see them. I thought about clouds, but the sky was so clear I saw no more. This special star was straight ahead in my vision down the road. It was so bright that I could not decide which was more spectacular, the sunset or the star. It twinkled brightly, and then as I made turns it seemed to turn with me. It looked like it was staying with me all the way.

I continued on my twenty mile trip back to my home enjoying the quiet music and the interesting combination of star and sunset.

Bright stars are in the sky all the time, but this one caught my attention since it was the only one there. There are thousands of stars in the sky, and I usually look at them and say how pretty they are. I do not focus on them for too long. I watched this star for thirty minutes. That was a record in star-watching for me. It represented light, company, and comfort while I was driving.

I wondered what all the other people on the road were thinking. Were they seeing the one star, and if so did it mean anything to them? Were they busy going somewhere? Did they see it? It was an intense bright starlight. Some might not have paid attention, but I noticed. I began to think about the importance of one light in the night sky. That star traveled with me, and I felt guided by it. When I arrived at my home and got out of the car, I looked up. There it was right where I live. I know the sky is a big place, and it is hard to follow where the constellations are. But for this night, I appreciated that light going home with me. I hope I can do the same for someone someday.

Printed in the United States
By Bookmasters